Lost Railways of the Lothians

by
Gordon Stansfield

The well-tended gardens at North Berwick Station, which is still open today.

Text © Gordon Stansfield, 2003.
First published in the United Kingdom, 2003,
by Stenlake Publishing Ltd,
Telephone / Fax: 01290 551122
Printed by Cordfall Ltd, Glasgow G21 2QA

ISBN 1 84033 270 0

The publishers regret that they cannot supply
copies of any pictures featured in this book.

PICTURE ACKNOWLEDGEMENTS
The publishers wish to thank the following for contributing photographs to this book: Hugh Brodie for the front cover, pages 6, 7, 9, 11, 19, 20, 26, 29, 30, 35, 38, 44, 45, 48, the inside back cover and the back cover; W.A.C. Smith for pages 4, 5, 10, 12, 23, 15, 18, 23–25, 28 (upper), 31–33, 36, 37, 41–43 and 47 (both).

The Forth Bridge, looking north towards the Fife coast.

INTRODUCTION

The Lothians comprise the counties of West, Mid and East Lothian, the combined area of which has had a considerable railway network over the years. It was in Edinburgh that the majority of railway developments took place. The first railway came to the city in 1832, when a passenger service began in the St Leonards area. Over the remainder of the nineteenth century new lines and stations opened and virtually every small village eventually had its own railway station.

It is difficult today to appreciate just how important the railways were. Every station had a handful of staff ranging from signalmen to porters, and the stationmaster was an important person in local communities. In the days before the coming of the motor car everything came by rail – from milk to racing pigeons. For the ordinary person in the street the railways opened up new horizons in work and leisure, allowing people to travel much further afield than ever before.

Competition between railway companies, especially the North British and the Caledonian who were prominent in the Lothians, was rife and in many cases lines were built which were never really viable. The Leith area of Edinburgh is a prime example of over-capacity as the North British built a grand station at Leith Central which never realised its full potential. The Caledonian also built stations and lines, some of which never saw a passenger train.

In the country areas of the three counties, passenger services tended to flourish until the coming of the motor bus from the 1920s onwards. Some services disappeared in the 1930s, but most lasted until the 1960s before being swept away for good. Edinburgh especially suffered this fate, with virtually all local suburban services disappearing. However, some have been reinstated such as those on the Bathgate line to Edinburgh and it is hoped that part of the Waverley route towards Galashiels will be reopened.

The Lothians' railways can be credited with some notable achievements and structures. Waverley Station in Edinburgh and the Forth Bridge are just two examples, but gone forever are others such as the Caledonian's Princes Street Station and oddities such as the station built at Granton Gasworks solely for the use of its employees.

It is hoped that this book will not only rekindle many fond memories of days gone by, but will also show to those who have never had the good fortune to experience widespread rail travel and that way of life just how important railways were to the people of the Lothians and Scotland as a whole.

Locomotives at St Margaret's Shed, Edinburgh.

Abbeyhill Junction – Piershill Junction Loop

Passenger service withdrawn	20 March 1988	*Stations closed*	*Date*
Distance	1 mile	Abbeyhill	7 September 1964
Company	North British	Piershill	7 September 1964

Abbeyhill Station on 21 August 1964, with a diesel multiple unit twin forming the 2.12 p.m. from Musselburgh to Edinburgh Waverley.

Abbeyhill Junction was the first junction reached after leaving Waverley Station on the east coast main line between Edinburgh and Berwick-upon-Tweed. It opened in 1868 and allowed train services operated by the North British Railway Company to reach Leith, with terminals at Leith Central, South Leith and North Leith. Abbeyhill Station was opened on 1 May 1869 and a junction was installed just past the station to provide a loop which rejoined the east coast main line at Piershill. Both Abbeyhill and Piershill stations handled suburban train services to and from Edinburgh Waverley. These services went to a variety of destinations – Leith, Musselburgh and North Berwick. Intermediate stations on the main line to Berwick were also served from Abbeyhill and Piershill. In addition there was a service known as the Edinburgh circular service. Starting at Waverley Station this service served Abbeyhill, Piershill, Portobello and then made its way through the southern Edinburgh suburbs before reaching Haymarket and then Waverley stations. Piershill Station was closed from January 1917 until April 1919 for reasons of wartime economy. Services calling at Abbeyhill and Piershill were withdrawn in 1964, although the line was retained for passenger trains which needed to detour from the short section of the east coast main line. The stations were purely for passenger use and never handled goods traffic.

Airdrie South – Ratho (Newbridge Junction) *

Passenger service withdrawn	9 January 1956		*Stations closed*	*Date*
Distance	25 miles		Bathgate Upper	9 January 1956
Company	North British		Livingstone	1 November 1948
			Uphall **	9 January 1956
Stations closed	*Date*		Drumshoreland ***	18 June 1951
Westcraigs	9 January 1956		Broxburn Junction	12 November 1849
Armadale	9 January 1956			

D34 No. 62495, 'Glen Luss', passes Armadale with the 12.59 p.m. service from Hyndland to Bathgate on the last day of service, 7 January 1956.

The Edinburgh & Bathgate Railway opened their Ratho to Bathgate section in November 1849. The Bathgate & Coatbridge Railway then opened the remaining section to Coatbridge and on to Glasgow. Services to Coatbridge began in August 1862 and by April 1871 through services were in operation between Edinburgh and Glasgow. Although passenger services were withdrawn in 1956, seasonal services operated to various holiday locations until 1960. In 1952 the station at Airdrie South was renamed Airdrie and following the withdrawal of the Glasgow to Edinburgh via Bathgate services in 1956, Airdrie became the eastern terminus of local services from Glasgow Queen Street Low level. In November 1960 the services received a new lease of life when the Glasgow north electrified suburban services (known affectionately as the 'Blue Trains') were introduced, giving a fast, clean and efficient service to Glasgow, Balloch and Helensburgh. Twenty-nine years had to elapse before the line was extended further eastward to Drumgelloch in May 1989. In the east a passenger service was reintroduced from Ratho to Bathgate in March 1986, thus providing once again an Edinburgh–Bathgate service. It is hoped that at some point the line between Bathgate and Drumgelloch will be reinstated, thereby providing once again through services between Edinburgh and Glasgow via Bathgate.

* Closed stations on this line that were in Lanarkshire were Clarkston (Lanark), Plains, Caldercruix and Forrestfield.

** Known as Houston until 1 August 1865.
*** Known as Broxburn until May 1870.

Bathgate Upper Station, *c.*1915.

Balerno – Ravelrig (Ravelrig Junction)

Passenger service withdrawn	11 September 1939
Distance	1.25 miles
Company	Caledonian

This line was built under the Caledonian Railway (Additional Powers) Act, 1870. It joined the main Caledonian line from Carstairs to Edinburgh Princes Street at Ravelrig Junction Station (which had two platforms). The short branch was beyond Balerno Station and created a loop which at the Edinburgh end left the line from Edinburgh Princes Street to Carstairs at Slateford before rejoining at Ravelrig Junction. As there were no stations on the line virtually no passenger trains used it. The odd train did run beyond Balerno to Ravelrig Junction Platform but this station was so remote that it closed in July 1920 (latterly, it served a local golf course). However the short branch was useful to the railway authorities over the years due to its remoteness and was a favourite location to keep the royal train when the royal family were visiting Edinburgh.

Balerno – Slateford (Balerno Junction)

		Stations closed	Date
Passenger service withdrawn	1 November 1943		
Distance	4.5 miles	Balerno	1 November 1943
Company	Caledonian	Currie	1 November 1943
		Juniper Green	1 November 1943
		Colinton	1 November 1943
		Hailes Halt	1 November 1943

Juniper Green Station, 19 September 1918.

Colinton Station.

The service from Balerno to Slateford continued onwards to Edinburgh's Princes Street Station after joining the Caledonian main line from Carstairs to Edinburgh. It opened to passengers on 1 August 1874. Most of the districts it passed through were residential, but as well as commuters the line carried many people on days out from Edinburgh, earning it the name of the 'picnic line'. At weekends many excursion trains were run to cope with the increased traffic. In order to stimulate growth the Caledonian's successor, the London, Midland & Scottish Railway, opened a halt at Hailes to cater for a local golf course. The line had very steep gradients and most of its rolling stock was made up of four-wheeled carriages. It was closed on 1 November 1943 as a wartime measure and although it was intended that the line reopen after the war, this never came about. The official closure date to passengers was 1 June 1949. Freight services ceased in 1967 and part of the former trackbed has since been converted to a walkway.

Bangour – Uphall (Bangour Asylum Branch Junction)

Passenger service withdrawn	4 May 1921	*Stations closed*	*Date*
Distance	1.5 miles	Bangour	4 May 1921
Company	North British	Dechmont	4 May 1921

Bangour Station.

Known as the Bangour Asylum Railway, this line was opened in 1905 after being authorised as a private railway by the Edinburgh District Lunacy Board. It was built to serve Bangour Asylum and provided virtually the only means of access for patients, visitors and supplies. The North British Railway operated the line and the station terminus at Bangour was shown in the public timetable as Bangour (Private). The intermediate station at Dechmont served the small village of the same name which housed many of the hospital's employees. Once road access to the hospital improved the need for a railway diminished. Freight services were withdrawn three months after passenger services ceased.

Barnton – Craigleith (Barnton Junction)

		Stations closed	Date
Passenger service withdrawn	7 May 1951	Barnton	7 May 1951
Distance	2.75 miles	Davidson's Mains	7 May 1951
Company	Caledonian	House O' Hill Halt	7 May 1951

The exterior of the former Barnton Station, 28 April 1962.

This branch line left the Princes Street to Leith and Newhaven line at Craigleith and opened to passenger traffic in March 1894. The Caledonian's original intention had been to extend the branch from Barnton southwards to provide a loop and make an inroad into newly developing residential areas. For various reasons this never came about. There were originally only two stations on the line and both were initially known by different names. Barnton was called Cramond Brig and Davidson's Mains was called Barnton Gate until 1 April 1903. An additional halt was opened in February 1937 at House O' Hill to cater for new suburban developments.

Blackston (Blackston Junction) – Bathgate Upper (Central Junction)

Passenger service withdrawn	1 May 1930	*Stations closed*		*Date*
Distance	4.75 miles	Westfield		1 May 1930
Company	North British	Bathgate Lower		1 May 1930

The closed Westfield Station, looking south, 18 April 1959.

The line from Blackston to Bathgate was a branch of the Monkland Railway and opened to passengers in 1856. It left the line from Airdrie to Manuel and Bo'ness at Blackston before heading south-east towards Bathgate where there were two stations – Bathgate Upper and Bathgate Lower. Bathgate Upper was the main junction station in this industrial area. In the 1920s trains could be taken east to Edinburgh, south to Whitburn and Morningside, west to Airdrie and Glasgow and north to Bo'ness. Bathgate's last passenger service was withdrawn on 9 January 1956, but in the late 1980s British Rail reintroduced a service between Edinburgh and the town. On average there were about eight return workings daily on the line between Blackston and Bathgate, with trains originating either at Coatbridge or Manuel. The last passenger train to use the line was a rail tour special on 19 June 1962 pulled by the locomotive *Glen Douglas* which is now preserved in Glasgow's Museum of Transport.

The closed Bathgate Lower Station, looking north, 20 March 1954.

Bo'ness – Manuel (Bo'ness High Junction)

Passenger service withdrawn	7 May 1956	*Stations closed*	*Date*
Distance	4 miles	Bo'ness	7 May 1956
Company	North British	Kinniel	22 September 1930

In 1849 the Monkland Railway Company announced that Bo'ness on the Firth of Forth would have a railway link to Airdrie and the Monklands. The attraction of Bo'ness was its harbour and the traffic it would generate, but this was not to be as nearby Grangemouth expanded and proved to be much better suited for this purpose. However, it was not until 1856 that the Monkland Railway Company reached Bo'ness and in 1865 it was taken over by the North British. Although services were provided by the North British, Bo'ness town council were keen to see their harbour developed. The North British were approached in order to fund the harbour redevelopment but it declined so the council approached a rival railway company, the Caledonian, which had been given permission to run some of their services over the line. Unfortunately, they too were unwilling to finance the development. Services from Bo'ness ran to Manuel Low Level Station and onwards to Airdrie but these were withdrawn in 1933. The remaining services, which lasted until 1956, ran from Bo'ness to the present day Polmont Station on the Edinburgh to Glasgow line via Falkirk High. Kinniel Station closed for two years during the First World War as an economy measure. Today passengers can still travel this line as most of it is used by the Scottish Railway Preservation Society and is known as the Bo'ness & Kinniel Railway. Steam services run from Bo'ness to Birkhill although the line continues as far as the Edinburgh to Glasgow main line where future proposals include the building of a station at Manuel.

Canal Street – Trinity Junction

Passenger service withdrawn	2 March 1868	*Stations closed*	*Date*
Distance	1.75 miles	Canal Street	2 March 1868
Company	Edinburgh, Perth & Dundee	Scotland Street	2 March 1868

An 0-6-0 locomotive, No. 1, which was built between 1865 and 1875, at the closed Scotland Street Station, Edinburgh.

Although this line was built by the Edinburgh, Leith & Granton Railway Company the company was originally known as the Edinburgh, Leith & Newhaven Railway Company when proposals were first put forward for its construction in the late 1830s. By the time of closure in 1868 the name had changed again to the Edinburgh, Perth & Dundee Railway Company. The line was opened on 31 August 1842 from Canal Street Station, which had two platforms, and the initial part of the journey was made through a tunnel which emerged at Scotland Street Station. The North British Railway Company made an inroad into Leith in 1860, and with the opening up of a link from Abbeyhill the service from Canal Street was discontinued as the North British route ran direct to Waverley Station. The tunnel at Scotland Street was closed along with Scotland Street and Canal Street stations. It was subsequently used for mushroom growing and a proposal was subsequently put forward to convert it into an underground car park, although this never came to fruition.

Corstorphine – Haymarket West Junction

Passenger service withdrawn	1 January 1968	*Stations closed*	*Date*
Distance	2 miles	Corstorphine	1 January 1968
Company	North British	Pinkhill	1 January 1968
		Balgreen Halt	1 January 1968

Class V3 2-6-2T No. 67617 arrives at Pinkhill Station with the 11.10 a.m. from Corstorphine to North Berwick, 14 December 1957.

The railway didn't arrive at Corstorphine until February 1902 and when it did it came in a way that was not really planned. In the latter part of the nineteenth century the Caledonian Railway Company drew up proposals to extend its Barnton branch line towards the North British Edinburgh to Glasgow route (the one still in use today between Edinburgh and Glasgow Queen Street). It intended to turn eastwards just before reaching the North British line, continuing through Corstorphine and providing a circular service. For several reasons this plan fell through and all Corstorphine ended up with was a branch line which began just west of Haymarket Station. Originally Pinkhill was the only intermediate station but in January 1934 the London & North Eastern Railway Company opened a halt at Balgreen. Pinkhill Station was closed as a wartime economy measure between January 1917 and February 1919. Services from Corstorphine were extended in the 1960s when British Railways ran trains to Musselburgh and North Berwick. In the last years services were a mixture of steam and diesel multiple units, with the journey to Edinburgh's Waverley Station taking fifteen minutes. Only Corstorphine had freight facilities and these survived a month longer than the passenger service.

Dalkeith – Eskbank (Glenesk Junction)

Passenger service withdrawn	5 January 1942	*Station closed*	*Date*
Distance	2 miles	Dalkeith	5 January 1942
Company	North British		

Although this short branch line ended up as a link from Dalkeith to the Waverley route from Edinburgh to Carlisle, it was originally the terminus of the Edinburgh and Dalkeith line which operated from the capital under a different gauge. By 1847 the North British Railway had converted the line to the standard gauge and connected it to the Waverley route. For wartime economy reasons it was closed to passengers from January 1917 until October 1919. Service levels by the mid-1920s were minimal, with just three return workings Monday to Saturday. After passenger services were withdrawn the line remained in use for freight traffic until August 1964 although a railtour special did visit the line in August 1962. The station was demolished in the 1960s and the site acquired by the Scottish Transport Group. One of their bus operating subsidiaries, Scottish Omnibuses Limited, whose fleet name was Eastern Scottish, built a new bus station and garage on the site which came into use in the late 1960s.

Dalmeny (North Junction) – Winchburgh (Winchburgh Junction)

Passenger service withdrawn	1 January 1973
Distance	3 miles
Company	North British

This branch linked the Edinburgh to Glasgow via Falkirk line with the Edinburgh to Dundee line via the Forth Bridge, which opened in March 1890. There were no intermediate stations on the line. With nationalisation in the early 1970s and the withdrawal of direct services between Glasgow and towns such as Kirkcaldy and Leven, the line was no longer required for passenger traffic. The last scheduled passenger service to use the line was the 7.07 a.m. from Thornton Junction to Glasgow Queen Street, with the return working leaving Glasgow at 5.09 p.m. Although the line remains in use for freight services a peak hour only service from Kirkcaldy to Glasgow was reintroduced in the late 1990s but was subsequently withdrawn.

Fisherrow – Fisherrow Junction

Passenger service withdrawn	15 July 1847	*Station closed*	*Date*
Distance	0.75 miles	Fisherrow	15 July 1847
Company	Edinburgh & Dalkeith		

Fisherrow was a small village on the west bank of the River Esk when the railway first arrived. It lay across the river from the town of Musselburgh, which at that time did not have a railway. The line to Fisherrow ran from Niddrie and train services were in operation by 1831. However, when the North British opened the line from Fisherrow Junction to Musselburgh, the station at Fisherrow was closed. Freight services continued to use the line until October 1961, by which time the goods depot was known as Fisherrow Siding.

Fisherrow Junction – Niddrie (North Junction)

Passenger service withdrawn	16 May 1859
Distance	1 mile
Company	Edinburgh & Dalkeith

This line was part of the route from Niddrie to Fisherrow. A branch from Fisherrow Junction to Musselburgh was opened to passengers on 16 July 1847, but as there was no connection to the east coast main line at New Hailes until 1859 trains had to continue on the Edinburgh & Dalkeith's line to Niddrie before proceeding to Edinburgh. When a junction at New Hailes was installed there was no need for trains to use the old line.

Galashiels (Kilnknowe Junction) – Rosewell and Hawthornden *

Passenger service withdrawn	5 February 1952	*Stations closed*	*Date*
Distance	37 miles	Leadburn	7 November 1955
Company	North British	Pomathorn Halt	5 February 1962
		Rosslynlee Hospital Halt	5 February 1962
		Rosslynlee	5 February 1962

* Closed stations on this line that were in Selkirkshire were Clovenfords and Thornielee. Closed stations in Peeblesshire were Walkerburn, Innerleithen, Cardrona, Peebles (first), Peebles East, Earlyvale Gate and Eddleston.

Leadburn Station.

The 12.21 p.m. diesel multiple unit from Edinburgh Waverley to Galashiels via Peebles arrives at Pomathorn Halt, 20 January 1962.

The line to Rosewell and Hawthornden was a wide loop which left the Waverley route at Galashiels and opened in 1866. Being quite long, the loop had a number of lines radiating from it. At Peebles there was the Caledonian line to Symington which closed in June 1950. At Leadburn was a junction station with a line going westwards to Carstairs. However this line was in two sections for operating purposes, each run by a separate company. From Leadburn to Dolphinton the North British had responsibility, withdrawing its service on 1 April 1933, while at the western end the Caledonian operated services from Dolphinton to Carstairs. These lasted until 12 September 1932 but were reinstated from 17 July 1933 until 2 June 1945. Needless to say each company had its own station at Dolphinton. At Rosewell and Hawthornden there was a branch to Penicuik which closed in September 1951. Rosslynlee Hospital Halt was opened in British Railways' days. The service along the route was very sparse; in 1948 there were three return journeys from Edinburgh to Galashiels Mondays to Fridays. On Saturdays there were two extra from Edinburgh, but only one from Galashiels. Freight services were withdrawn on the same date as passenger services.

Gifford – Monktonhall Junction

Passenger service withdrawn	3 April 1933	*Stations closed*	*Date*
Distance	15 miles	Saltoun	3 April 1933
Company	North British	Pencaitland	3 April 1933
		Ormiston	3 April 1933
Stations closed	*Date*	Crossgatehall Halt	22 September 1930
Gifford	3 April 1933	Smeaton	22 September 1930
Humbie	3 April 1933		

Gifford Station.

Saltoun Station.

The line from Gifford to Edinburgh joined the east coast main line at Monktonhall Junction and provided a through service from East Lothian to the city. There were two junctions on the line. At Smeaton there was a line to Hardengreen Junction on the Waverley route, although this did not carry passenger traffic. There was a short branch line to Macmerry at Ormiston which closed in July 1925. The line opened as far as Macmerry in May 1872 and the section from Ormiston to Gifford was operational by October 1901. This was a light railway and as such had various restrictions placed on it, including speed limits: the nine-and-a-quarter mile trip from Gifford to Ormiston took half an hour. Until the Macmerry branch closed, some of the trains joined at Ormiston to form a through train to Edinburgh. The total journey time from Gifford to Edinburgh was about an hour. Crossgatehall Halt was closed from 1 January 1917 until 1 February 1919 as a wartime economy measure.

Glencorse – Millerhill (Millerhill Junction)

Passenger service withdrawn	1 May 1933	*Stations closed*	*Date*
Distance	8 miles	Glencorse	1 May 1933
Company	North British	Roslin	1 May 1933
		Loanhead	1 May 1933
		Gilmerton	1 May 1933

The viaduct at Glencorse.

Loanhead Station.

The line from Glencorse in the south of Edinburgh joined the Waverley route at Millerhill. The part of the route from Millerhill to Roslin was opened by the Edinburgh, Loanhead & Roslin Railway in July 1874 and the line was extended to Glencorse three years later. This was one of several branch lines in the area and provided a through service to Edinburgh Waverley or Leith Central – there were four to five return workings to Edinburgh with additional trains on Saturdays. The line fared well in the days before road transport began to seriously erode passenger numbers. Gilmerton Station was closed from 1 January 1917 until 2 June 1919 except for workmen's trains. Although passenger services were withdrawn in 1933 the line continued to carry freight traffic until 1959, with trains travelling as far as Loanhead until 1968. Specials visited the line too and the North British locomotive *Glen Douglas*, now preserved in Glasgow's Museum of Transport, made its first trip along the line after its restoration.

Granton East – Powderhall (Bonnington South Junction)

Passenger service withdrawn	2 November 1925	*Stations closed*	*Date*
Distance	2 miles	Granton East	2 November 1925
Company	North British	Trinity and Newhaven	2 November 1925

The closed station of Trinity & Newhaven, 7 April 1958.

Opened in February 1846, the station at Granton East handled some of the earliest boat trains to run from Edinburgh. The Forth railway bridge had not yet been built, and trains ran from Canal Street Station to Granton to connect with steamer services to Burntisland. With the demise of the steamer services Granton lost much of its importance and became the terminus of a suburban branch line. The station was officially called Granton East and in the early 1900s trains ran to Waverley Station via Abbeyhill, the four-and-a-half mile trip taking fifteen minutes. At Bonnington South Junction this line joined the one from North Leith (which remained in use until June 1947). The Granton line was closed to passengers from January 1917 until February 1919 as a wartime economy measure. By the early 1920s traffic levels were much reduced, resulting in only about eight trains daily from Granton. The line remained *in situ* for many years after closure and one of the last passenger trains which used the line was a special in 1967.

Granton Gasworks – Granton (Crewe Junction)

Passenger service withdrawn	1942	*Station closed*	*Date*
Distance	1 mile	Granton Gasworks	1942
Company	Caledonian		

The closed station at Granton Gasworks, 21 May 1955.

Granton Gasworks Station was used solely by the employees of Granton Gasworks, with the Caledonian providing special trains which ran to and from Princes Street. The passenger service ceased in 1942, although the gasworks continued to have a freight service until 1986.

Gullane – Longniddry (Aberlady Junction)

Passenger service withdrawn	12 September 1932	*Stations closed*	*Date*
Distance	4.75 miles	Gullane	12 September 1932
Company	North British	Luffness	1 June 1931
		Aberlady	12 September 1932

Gullane was reached by a branch line which left the east coast main line at Longniddry and headed northwards. Opened in April 1898, it was hoped that the line would continue beyond Gullane to North Berwick, but this proposal never came to fruition and the line had to make do with branch status. It did, however, boast a named train – the Lothian Coast Express – which ran direct to Edinburgh and Glasgow from Gullane as well as carrying portions from Dunbar and North Berwick. There was a return working in the late afternoon. The express took three quarters of an hour to reach Edinburgh and a further hour to reach Glasgow. Most local trains consisted of just one coach. Luffness Station was established for the golf course there. Freight services lasted thirty-two years after passenger services were withdrawn and specials visited the line from time to time. One of the last was in June 1960.

A Stephenson Locomotive Society 'East Lothian Excursion' visits the closed Aberlady Station, 11 June 1960.

Haddington – Longniddry (Longniddry Junction)

Passenger service withdrawn	5 December 1949	*Station closed*	*Date*
Distance	4.75 miles	Haddington	5 December 1949
Company	North British		

In its early proposals for the east coast main line between Edinburgh and Berwick upon Tweed, the North British Railway Company wanted to run the line via Haddington, but due to engineering difficulties the route was altered and Haddington ended up as a branch line terminus. The line ran from Longniddry on the present-day east coast main line and opened to passengers in 1846. The North British provided through trains to Edinburgh and even had the branch constructed as double track, although it was reduced to single track a few years after opening. There were about ten return journeys on weekdays, with the trip to Haddington from Longniddry taking about ten minutes. The line was one of the first to be closed in Scotland by British Railways. Before final services took place in 1968 various specials travelled the branch line, the last one being a diesel multiple unit in 1967.

Kershope Foot – Portobello East Junction *

Passenger service withdrawn	6 January 1969	*Stations closed*	*Date*
Distance	74 miles	Fushiebridge	4 October 1943
Company	North British	Gorebridge	6 January 1969
		Newtongrange	6 January 1969
Stations closed	*Date*	Dalhousie	1 August 1908
Bowland	7 December 1953	Eskbank & Dalkeith	6 January 1969
Stow	6 January 1969	Glenesk	1 November 1917
Fountainhall	6 January 1969	Millerhill	7 November 1955
Heriot	6 January 1969	Niddrie	1 February 1869
Tynehead	6 January 1969	Niddrie Junction	15 July 1847

Fountainhall Station.

* The closed station on this line that was in Cumberland was Kershope Foot. The closed stations in Roxburghshire were Newcastleton, Steele Road, Riccarton Junction, Shankend, Stobs, Hawick (first), Hawick (second), Hassendean, Belses, St Boswells, Newstead and Melrose. The closed station in Selkirkshire was Galashiels.

Heriot Station.

The line from Kershope Foot to Edinburgh formed the northerly section of the Waverley route. Operating it was difficult because of the line's severe gradients and numerous curves and twists. One of the remotest stations on the line was at Riccarton Junction (known as Riccarton until January 1905), where a station and community was created by the North British Railway in order to service the route. There was no road access to the community of about thirty cottages. The remote nature of the settlement caused friction and in several instances the police had to be called in to maintain law and order. The Waverley route had numerous branches radiating from it both to the west and east. On a wintry Sunday night in January 1969 the overnight sleeper service from Edinburgh Waverley to London St Pancras marked the end of passenger services on the route. Anti-closure protesters blocked the line at Newcastleton Station for more than an hour, but to no avail. Proposals for reopening part of the Waverley route are under consideration and it is likely that within the next few years towns such as Galashiels will once again have a rail service.

A Type 2 diesel locomotive arriving at Gorebridge with the 4.10 p.m. service from Edinburgh Waverley to Hawick, 11 May 1963.

Lauder – Fountainhall Junction

Passenger service withdrawn	12 September 1932	*Stations closed*	*Date*
Distance	10.25 miles	Lauder	12 September 1932
Company	North British	Oxton	12 September 1932

In July 1901 the Lauder Light Railway opened between Fountainhall Junction and Lauder, with one intermediate station at Oxton. Prior to this a subsidised bus service had operated between Stow Station on the Waverley route and Lauder. The line was one of several short-lived light railways that opened in Scotland around the start of the twentieth century. In this case the passenger service lasted until 1932 whilst freight traffic continued until 1958. The branch line was fairly steeply graded in some sections and for years a service of three return journeys (four on Saturdays) ran between Lauder and Fountainhall Junction. From there passengers could continue northwards to Edinburgh or south in the direction of Galashiels. The line provided a proper transport infrastructure in this part of the country and helped to open up the area to new trade. Fishermen, for instance, were given access to the large trout streams which the area is famous for. In November 1958 a steam special travelled the branch shortly before the track was lifted.

Oxton Station, *c*.1909.

Leadburn (Leadburn Junction) – Dolphinton

Passenger service withdrawn	1 April 1933
Distance	10 miles
Company	North British

Although this line originated at Leadburn in Midlothian, the other stations on it were in Peeblesshire (Lamancha, Macbiehill and Broomlee) and Lanarkshire (Dolphinton). The line was built by the Leadburn, Linton & Dolphinton Railway Company and opened to passenger traffic in July 1864. There were six return journeys on weekdays and eight on Saturdays, with the ten mile trip to Dolphinton taking just under half an hour. Freight services were also withdrawn in April 1933 and the line was lifted shortly afterwards.

Leith Central – Abbeyhill (London Road Junction)

Passenger service withdrawn	7 April 1952	*Station closed*	*Date*
Distance	1 mile	Leith Central	7 April 1952
Company	North British		

Leith Central Station, c.1908.

Leith Central Station opened to passenger traffic on 1 July 1903 and provided a half-hourly service to Edinburgh Waverley. The branch line terminus was one of several stations in the suburban area of Leith, where both the North British and Caledonian Railways had a presence. Rivalry between the two companies was what led to Leith Central being opened. Its signal box was so extensive that it had eighty-one levers, and the grand station is understood to have been the largest to be built from scratch in the twentieth century. Due to lack of publicity about its local services to Edinburgh city centre, a lot of potential passenger traffic was lost to other rival transport operators such as the tramway companies and bus operators. The station was much too big for the traffic it handled and even when a fire broke out in the 1930s damaging two platforms there was no disruption to services. Although only a mile in length, the line took two years to build. A junction at Lochend allowed trains to run via Duddingston on the Edinburgh suburban line to Waverley Station. After closure to passengers the line and station (minus platforms) were used as a servicing depot for diesel multiple units. These were first introduced in 1957 on the Edinburgh to Glasgow services and then on other suburban routes. The station continued to be used as a depot until 1972 and survived until 1999 when it was demolished to make way for a supermarket complex.

Leith North – Dalry Middle Junction

Passenger service withdrawn	30 April 1962	*Stations closed*	*Date*
Distance	5 miles	East Pilton	30 April 1962
Company	Caledonian	Craigleith	30 April 1962
		Murrayfield	30 April 1962
		Dalry Road	30 April 1962
Stations closed	*Date*		
Leith North *	30 April 1962		
Newhaven	30 April 1962	* Originally known as Leith. Renamed North Leith on 1 August 1903	
Granton Road	30 April 1962	and Leith North on 7 April 1952.	

A diesel multiple unit forms the last ever departure from Leith North to Edinburgh Princes Street at 6.45 p.m on 28 April 1962.

Edinburgh Corporation tram No. 37 reversing on service 23
outside Granton Road Station, 16 November 1956.

This was one of the Caledonian's suburban services with trains running to and from their terminus at Princes Street Station. When the first passenger service was introduced in August 1879 trains ran to Lothian Road Station, the predecessor to Princes Street. As with many other suburban services, competition from trams and buses in the early twentieth century threatened this line. However, attempts were made to stimulate traffic, with the London, Midland & Scottish Railway Company opening a halt at East Pilton on 1 December 1934 (the 'halt' was dropped in November 1938). Newhaven, Granton Road, East Pilton and Dalry Road stations were purely passenger stations and had no freight facilities. In the 1930s the journey time for the five-and-a-half mile trip to Princes Street was twenty minutes, with about twenty-five return trips being provided on weekdays. The number had dropped to about sixteen by the early 1950s. The last passenger services were operated by diesel multiple units and after closure the line was quickly lifted.

Class V3 2-6-2T No. 67624 starts away from Dalry Road Station with the 1.10 p.m. from Leith North to Edinburgh Princes Street, 19 March 1960.

Lochend Junction – Lochend North Junction

Passenger service withdrawn	7 April 1952
Distance	0.25 miles
Company	North British

This short branch line was built to enable trains from Leith Central to join the line from Granton, thereby providing an alternative route from Leith Central to Edinburgh Waverley via Piershill, Portobello and the Edinburgh suburban circle. Leith Central Station was opened on 1 July 1903 and by October of that year the branch was in use. Trains began and ended their journey at Leith Central with outer circle trains travelling via Piershill and inner circle ones via Abbeyhill. After the withdrawal of passenger services, Leith Central continued to be used as a service point for diesel multiple units and locomotives until 1972 and the branch was also used for empty coach workings.

Lothian Road – Dalry East Junction

Passenger service withdrawn	2 May 1870	*Station closed*	*Date*
Distance	0.25 miles	Lothian Road	2 May 1870
Company	Caledonian		

Opened on 15 February 1848, Lothian Road Station was the Caledonian Railway's first terminus in Edinburgh and catered for their trains from Carlisle and Glasgow Central via Shotts. The terminus was very cramped, and as the Caledonian were eager to expand further towards Princes Street they switched terminuses when they opened their new Princes Street Station in May 1870. Lothian Road continued to be used as a freight depot.

Macmerry – Ormiston (Ormiston Junction)

Passenger service withdrawn	1 July 1925	*Stations closed*	*Date*
Distance	2.5 miles	Macmerry	1 July 1925
Company	North British	Winton	1 July 1925

This line formed the northern part of the route from Macmerry to Edinburgh which joined the east coast main line at Monktonhall Junction. Ormiston was a junction station from where trains ran on a light railway to Gifford. Trains either combined or divided at Ormiston, depending on which direction they were going in. There were two return workings from Macmerry with an additional journey on Saturdays. Although the last scheduled passenger service ran in 1925 a steam special visited the line in 1958 when the route was still open to freight traffic. When freight services were withdrawn in March 1960 the line closed completely.

Manuel Low Level – Bo'ness Low Junction *

Passenger service withdrawn	1 May 1933
Distance	0.75 miles
Company	North British

This line formed part of the route from Bo'ness to Coatbridge. At Bo'ness Low Junction the line divided with one branch joining the Edinburgh to Glasgow main line and the other branch continuing south under the main line to Manuel Low Level Station. Manuel High Level Station was on the Edinburgh to Glasgow main line, while the low level station was on the Bo'ness to Coatbridge line. Services from the low level station were withdrawn in May 1930. Although the line was built in 1851 it was not until five years later that passenger services began with through trains from Coatbridge to Manuel and onwards to Bo'ness, although these through services were withdrawn in the 1890s. After the withdrawal of passenger services between Coatbridge and Manuel a shuttle service remained for traffic between Manuel Low Level and Bo'ness. The high level station continued to be used until 1967 and right up until that time booking office facilities were provided at the low level station. The passenger service was not very good in the line's last years, with only five return workings provided between Manuel and Bo'ness. No freight service facilities were provided at the low level station.

* The one closed station on this line, Manuel Low Level, was in Stirlingshire.

Morningside – Bathgate (Polkemmet South Junction) *

Passenger service withdrawn	1 May 1930	*Stations closed*	*Date*
Distance	13.75 miles	Bents	1 May 1930
Company	North British	Whitburn	1 May 1930

Stations closed	*Date*
Fauldhouse & Crofthead	1 May 1930

* Closed stations on this line that were in Lanarkshire were Morningside, Blackhall and Headless Cross.

Fauldhouse & Crofthead Station, *c.*1912.

Morningside formed the boundary between two railway companies. The Caledonian and the North British were succeeded by the London, Midland & Scottish and the London & North Eastern and the stations belonging to each company were situated as an end-on connection to each other. This area in West Lothian was a rich mineral eldorado for the railway companies and competition between the Caledonian and North British was very fierce there. The line from Morningside to Bathgate included part of the original 1843 Wishaw & Coltness Railway and was seen as a strong inroad into Caledonian territory by the North British Railway. In the mid-1920s there were three return workings to Bathgate with an additional one on Saturdays. Freight services lasted until the mid-1960s.

Musselburgh – Joppa (New Hailes Junction)

Passenger service withdrawn	7 September 1964	*Station closed*	*Date*
Distance	1.25 miles	Musselburgh	7 September 1964
Company	North British		

The exterior of Musselburgh Station, 28 August 1964.

A rail service between Musselburgh and Edinburgh began in July 1847. The branch joined the east coast main line at Joppa, where services continued to Waverley, Haymarket and at times Corstorphine on the branch line from Haymarket. Although the town lost its passenger service in 1964, a new Musselburgh station was opened on the east coast main line in 1988. In the early 1960s Musselburgh had a good passenger service with twenty-seven departures for Edinburgh on weekdays. After closure some specials visited the line, the last of them in August 1966.

North Leith – Abbeyhill (London Road Junction)

Passenger service withdrawn	16 June 1947	*Stations closed*	*Date*
Distance	2 miles	Junction Bridge	16 June 1947
Company	North British	Bonnington	16 June 1947
		Powderhall	1 January 1917
Stations closed	*Date*	Leith Walk	30 March 1930
North Leith	16 June 1947	Easter Road	16 June 1947

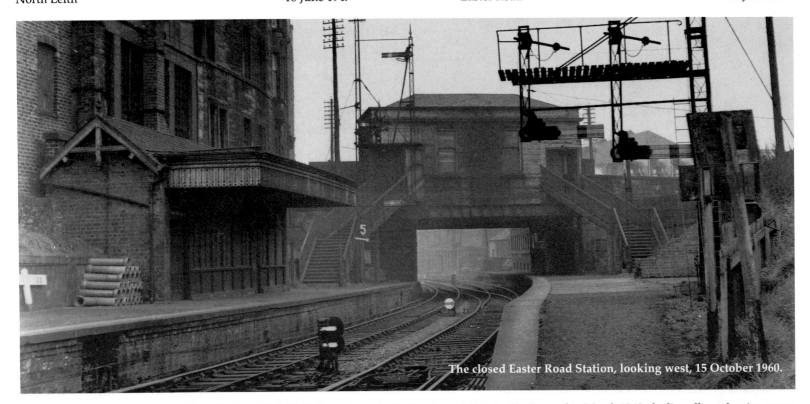

The closed Easter Road Station, looking west, 15 October 1960.

This suburban line was built to allow the North British Railway to make further inroads into Leith. Opened in March 1868, the line allowed trains to run direct into Waverley Station. North Leith was also known as Leith Citadel and all the stations on the line were closed from January 1917 until April 1919 (Powderhall never reopened). The closure of the line to passengers in 1947 was one of the last such decisions to be taken by the London & North Eastern Railway: competition from buses and trams had won the day. Part of the line is still in use and the platforms of some of the stations can still be made out.

Penicuik – Rosewell and Hawthornden (Hawthornden Junction)

Passenger service withdrawn	10 September 1951	*Stations closed*		*Date*
Distance	4.5 miles	Penicuik		10 September 1951
Company	North British	Eskbridge		22 September 1930
		Auchendinny		5 March 1951
		Rosslyn Castle		10 September 1951

Penicuik Station.

Auchendinny Station.

Penicuik acquired its first railway service in 1872 when a small independent company called the Penicuik Railway Company built this line. Trains ran to Edinburgh Waverley, joining the line from Galashiels to Edinburgh via Peebles and then the Waverley route. The sixteen mile trip to Edinburgh took about forty minutes. In 1949, two years before closure, trains left Penicuik at 7.32 a.m., 8.37 a.m., 3.16 p.m., 5.01 p.m. and on Saturdays only at 9.51 p.m. Eskbridge Station, which was closed from January 1917 until June 1919, was the only station on the line which had no freight facilities. Freight services lasted until March 1967 and a passenger special visited the line in August 1964. Today part of this route is used as a walkway and cycleway.

Polton – Eskbank (Esk Valley Junction)

Passenger service withdrawn	10 September 1951	*Stations closed*	*Date*
Distance	2.75 miles	Polton	10 September 1951
Company	North British	Lasswade	10 September 1951
		Broomieknowe	10 September 1951

The viaduct at Lasswade.

This short branch line provided suburban services to Edinburgh Waverley. It joined the Galashiels to Edinburgh via Peebles line at Esk Valley Junction, then the Waverley route at Hardengreen Junction. With improvements in road transport in the 1940s the level of passenger services was reduced quite significantly and in 1949 Polton had only five return journeys to Edinburgh with the eleven mile journey taking about half an hour. Broomieknowe Station was closed from January 1917 until April 1919 and had no freight facilities. Freight services from Polton and Lasswade were withdrawn in 1964 with the last passenger excursion travelling over the line in August 1963.

Port Edgar – South Queensferry Halt

Passenger service withdrawn	5 March 1890	*Stations closed*	*Date*
Distance	1.75 miles	Port Edgar	5 March 1890
Company	North British	South Queensferry	1 October 1878
		South Queensferry Halt	14 January 1929

Although authorised in June 1868, this line wasn't built until 1878. It remained in operation for passenger traffic until the opening of the Forth railway bridge on 4 March 1890 and formed part of a route which went via Kirkliston and joined the Edinburgh to Glasgow main line at Ratho. Ferry services to North Queensferry and onwards into Fife could be caught from Port Edgar. South Queensferry Station was closed in 1 October 1878 but resited nearby. It became known as South Queensferry Halt and reopened to passengers in 1919.

Portobello (Niddrie North Junction) – Haymarket Central Junction

Passenger service withdrawn	10 September 1962	*Stations closed*	*Date*
Distance	8 miles	Blackford Hill	10 September 1962
Company	North British	Morningside Road	10 September 1962
		Craiglockhart	10 September 1962
Stations closed	*Date*	Gorgie East *	10 September 1962
Duddingston	10 September 1962		
Newington	10 September 1962	* Known as Gorgie until May 1952.	

Class V1 2-6-2T No. 67608 at Morningside Road Station on 14 December 1957 with the 12.10 p.m. Outer Circle train from Edinburgh Waverley.

Class B1 4-6-0 No. 61117 at Gorgie East Station with a football special from Partick Hill, Glasgow, 2 February 1957.

In the 1880s and 1890s new parts of Edinburgh were undergoing residential development and it was to serve the transport needs of these areas that the Edinburgh, Suburban & Southside Junction Railway was opened on 1 December 1884. Services could be run from Waverley and back again as a circle operation or trains could bypass Waverley if required. Blackford Hill was the only station closed during the First World War. The line also carried trains from places beyond Edinburgh such as Musselburgh and Rosewell, and in its last days before closure had about sixteen trains in each direction. After closure to passengers in 1962 the line carried through passenger trains on Sundays until September 1964. It is still open for freight traffic.

Princes Street – Slateford Junction

Passenger service withdrawn	6 September 1965	*Stations closed*	*Date*
Distance	2.25 miles	Princes Street	6 September 1965
Company	Caledonian	Merchiston	10 September 1962

Class 4 2-6-4T No. 42172 leaves Merchiston Station with the 5.37 p.m. from Edinburgh Princes Street to Lanark, 16 July 1962.

Princes Street Station was the Caledonian's main line terminal in Edinburgh and the section from Princes Street to Slateford Junction carried trains to Glasgow via Shotts, Lanark, and main line services to Carlisle and the south. Some local services such as those to Granton used part of the route. In September 1964 a connecting line which had not previously been used by passenger trains was brought into use. This allowed trains which terminated at Princes Street to be rerouted at Slateford Junction to Haymarket and Waverley Stations. The last train to call at Princes Street was the 10.50 p.m. Saturday-only service from Glasgow Central which arrived on time at just after midnight. The last departure was the 11.30 p.m. to Birmingham. Today the only survivor of this nine platform main line station is the Caledonian Hotel which formed part of the station structure.

Ratho (Kirkliston Junction) – Dalmeny (South Junction)

Passenger service withdrawn	22 September 1930	*Stations closed*	*Date*
Distance	7 miles	Ratho Low Level Platform	22 September 1930
Company	North British	Kirkliston	22 September 1930

Kirkliston Station, *c.*1918.

Built to link with the ferry port of the Queensferry passage, this line opened in March 1866. However, the line was extended from Dalmeny to South Queensferry in 1868 to meet the requirements for a ferry passage across the Firth of Forth to Fife. The line lost a great deal of through passenger traffic when the Forth Bridge opened in 1890. This involved the construction of a more direct rail route from Edinburgh and left only local passenger traffic on the Ratho – Dalmeny line. Ratho had two stations – one on the Edinburgh to Glasgow line and the other on the Kirkliston line. The latter was known as Ratho Low Level Platform and had no freight facilities. Trains ran to and from Edinburgh Waverley with the journey time between there and Dalmeny being about forty-five minutes. Some trains continued to South Queensferry Halt and in the 1920s there were about five return workings daily.

Rosewell and Hawthornden – Eskbank (Hardengreen Junction)

Passenger service withdrawn	10 September 1962	*Stations closed*	*Date*
Distance	3 miles	Rosewell and Hawthornden *	10 September 1962
Company	North British	Bonnyrigg	10 September 1962

Bonnyrigg Station.

This was the last remaining section of line open to passengers on the route from Eskbank on the Waverley line to Galashiels via Peebles. The other section had closed in February 1962. The last timetable showed over twenty departures, with some journeys extending to the Corstorphine branch. Freight services to Bonnyrigg Station lasted until 1965.

* Known as Hawthornden until July 1928.

St Leonards – Duddingston (Duddingston Junction)

Passenger service withdrawn	30 September 1860	*Station closed*	*Date*
Distance	2 miles	St Leonards	30 September 1860
Company	Edinburgh & Dalkeith		

The branch line to St Leonards was opened in 1831 and handled trains from Edinburgh to Fisherrow, Dalkeith and Leith. It passed beneath the grounds of Holyrood Palace through a steep tunnel. On 1 November 1847 the station was closed, but it reopened in June 1860 for services to Dalkeith, closing to passengers again later in the year. The line remained open for goods traffic until August 1968. In the 1960s various railway specials visited the line including steam specials in 1962 and 1965. The site of the St Leonards branch remains in use to this day as part of a cycleway known as the 'Innocent Railway'. The name was derived from the railway's claim to have been very safe in its early days of operation and to have had no accidents, although this was not strictly true as some did happen to railway employees.

South Leith – Portobello (West Junction)

Passenger service withdrawn	2 January 1905	*Station closed*	*Date*
Distance	2 miles	South Leith	2 January 1905
Company	North British		

The South Leith branch originated at a junction on the east coast main line at Portobello. Leith was saturated with passenger stations, and at one time had five of them. The South Leith branch line was the first to lose its passenger service, mainly because it headed east away from Edinburgh. The line is still used today by freight services travelling to the docks at Leith. The North British's rival, the Caledonian, wanted a share of the Leith passenger traffic and had in fact built its own line with three stations in the same area as the North British. However it did a U-turn at the last moment and, despite having built three stations at Newhaven, Ferry Road and Leith Walk, never introduced a passenger service.

South Queensferry Halt – Dalmeny (South Junction)

Passenger service withdrawn	14 January 1929	*Stations closed*	*Date*
Distance	2 miles	South Queensferry Halt	14 January 1929
Company	North British	New Halls	1 September 1878
		Dalmeny (first) *	5 March 1890

The present Dalmeny Station, *c.*1900.

* A new station – Forth Bridge – was opened on a different site to replace this station on 5 March 1890. This was renamed Dalmeny on 28 April 1890 and is still open.

This line formed part of the route from Ratho Station to South Queensferry and Port Edgar. The section from Dalmeny to South Queensferry opened to passenger traffic on 1 June 1868, although New Halls Station didn't open until May 1870 and closed in September 1878. The line closed to passenger traffic on 5 March 1890, reopening on 1 December 1919. South Queensferry Station was resited in October 1878 and subsequently had its name changed to South Queensferry Halt. It also served as a goods station and continued to handle freight traffic until 1966.

Closed passenger stations on lines still open to passenger services

Line/Service   **Carstairs – Edinburgh***

Line/Service   **Edinburgh – Berwick upon Tweed***

Stations closed	Date
Jocks Lodge	1 July 1848
Portobello	7 September 1964

Stations closed	Date
Cobbinshaw (first)	4 October 1875
Cobbinshaw	18 April 1966
Harburn	18 April 1966
Ravelrig Platform	1 July 1920
Curriehill **	2 April 1951
Kingsknowe ***	6 July 1964

* Closed stations on this line that were in Lanarkshire were Carnwath and Auchengray.
** Reopened October 1987.
*** Closed from 1 January 1917 until 1 February 1919. Reopened 1 February 1971.

Class 4 2-6-4T No. 42273 draws into Kingsknowe Station with empty coaches to form the 1.23 p.m. to Edinburgh Princes Street, 29 February 1964.

Stations closed (continued)	Date
Joppa (first)	1859
Joppa	7 September 1964
Newhailes **	6 February 1950
Inveresk ***	4 May 1964
Wallyford	14 October 1867
Seton Mains Halt	22 September 1930
Ballencrieff	1 November 1847
East Fortune	4 May 1964
East Linton ****	4 May 1964
Innerwick	18 June 1951

* Closed stations on this line that were in Berwickshire were Cockburnspath, Grantshouse, Reston, Ayton and Burnmouth.
** Known as New Hailes until 26 September 1938.
*** Known as Musselburgh until May 1847, Inveresk until 1 October 1876 and Inveresk Junction until 2 June 1890.
**** Known as Linton until December 1864.

Class 3 2-6-2T No. 40159 at Portobello on 14 December 1957 with the 1.11 p.m. Outer Circle train from Edinburgh Waverley.

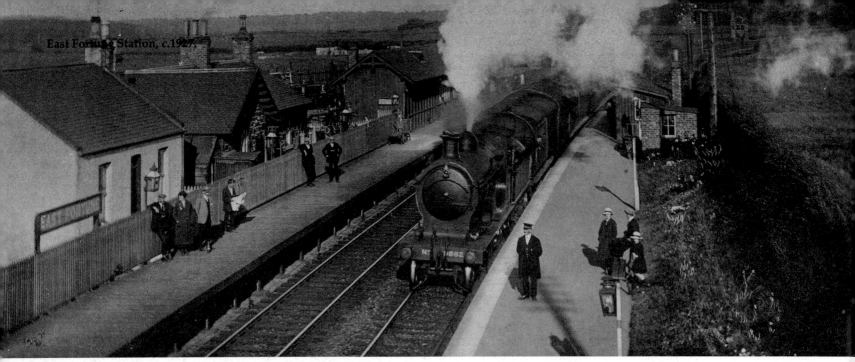

East Fortune Station, c.1927.